HOW'S YOUR HEALTH?

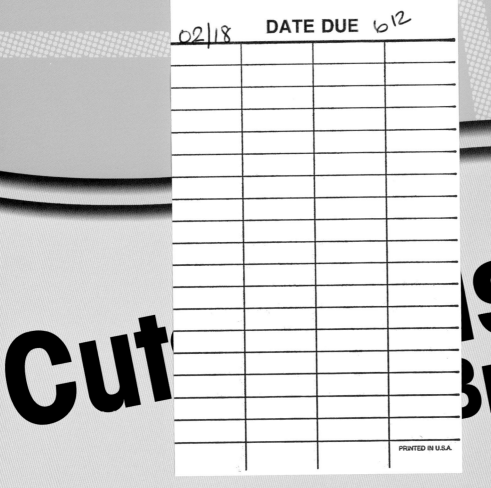
Cut ses Breaks

Angela Royston

F S

First published in 2006 by
Franklin Watts
338 Euston Road
London NW1 3BH

Franklin Watts Australia
Hachette Children's Books
Level 17/207 Kent Street
Sydney NSW 2000

Produced by Calcium, New Brook House, 385 Alfreton Road, Nottingham, NG7 5LR

Editor: Sarah Eason
Design: Paul Myerscough
Illustration: Annie Boberg and Geoff Ward
Picture research: Sarah Jameson
Consultant: Dr Stephen Earwicker

Acknowledgements:
The publisher would like to thank the following for permission to reproduce photographs:
Alamy p.9, p.11, p.16, p.17, p.20, p.21, p.23, p.25; Picture Library p.7; Inmagine p.19; CMSP
p.22; Corbis p.26; Tudor Photography p.8; Chris Fairclough Photography p.6, p.10, p.12,
p.13, p.15, p.27.

Every attempt has been made to clear copyright. Should there be any inadvertent omission
please apply to the publisher for rectification.

A CIP catalogue record for this book is available from the British Library.

Dewey Decimal Classification Number: 617.1

ISBN-10: 0 7496 6671 4
ISBN-13: 978 0 7496 6671 2

Printed in China

Franklin Watts is a division of Hachette Children's Books.

Contents

What are cuts, bruises and breaks?

Cuts, bruises and breaks are all **injuries** that hurt your body.

When you harm your skin, you bleed a little. If you cut or scrape your skin, blood oozes out through the **wound**. If the blood cannot escape, it becomes a bruise.

Things that can cause cuts, bruises and breaks:

+ Falling over and banging yourself can cause a cut, bruise or break.
+ People can accidentally cut themselves on sharp tools, such as knives and scissors.

If someone harms a bone, it may crack or break. Even a thin crack can be very painful. If a bone has a crack or a break it will be too painful to move normally. A **cast** protects the bone as it mends itself.

What is blood?

Blood is a red liquid that flows through tubes to every part of your body, except your hair and nails.

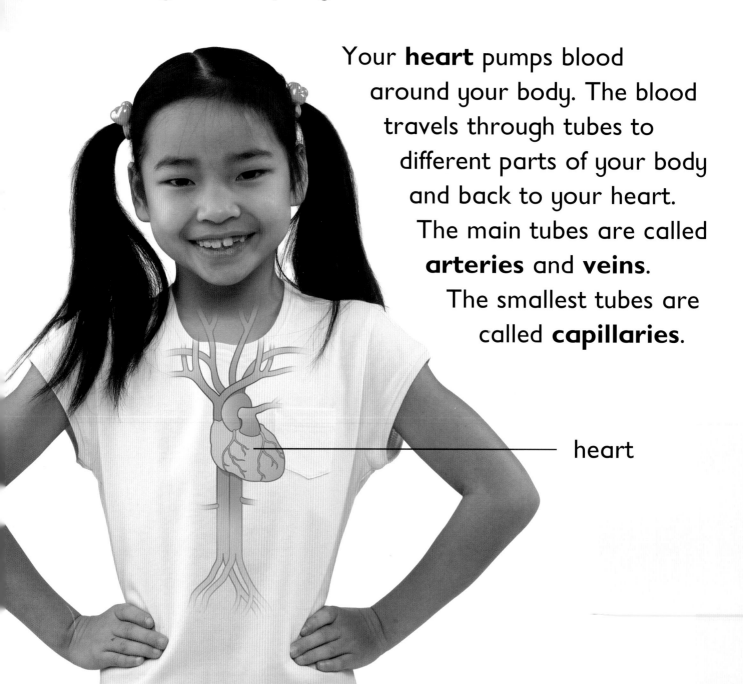

Your **heart** pumps blood around your body. The blood travels through tubes to different parts of your body and back to your heart. The main tubes are called **arteries** and **veins**. The smallest tubes are called **capillaries**.

heart

When skin is cut, some of the tiny capillaries in the skin are also cut. A small amount of blood leaks out from the capillaries and through the cut.

Carrying germs

+ Blood carries lots of things that your body needs, but it also carries **germs**.

+ Some germs are dangerous, which is why you shouldn't touch other people's blood.

How are cuts treated?

Cuts must be cleaned and then covered to keep out dirt.

Wash a cut under running water to clean away any dirt. Using an **antiseptic** cream will help to kill any germs. Cover the cut with a clean plaster that is large enough to cover the whole cut.

Try this!

If you tread on a hose of running water, the water should stop flowing. You can stop a cut bleeding in the same way:

1. Make sure the cut is completely clean.
2. Fold a piece of kitchen roll and press it over the cut for five minutes. The blood should stop running from the wound.

If a cut is deep, a nurse or doctor may have to **stitch** the wound. The stitches hold the edges of the cut together while it **heals**.

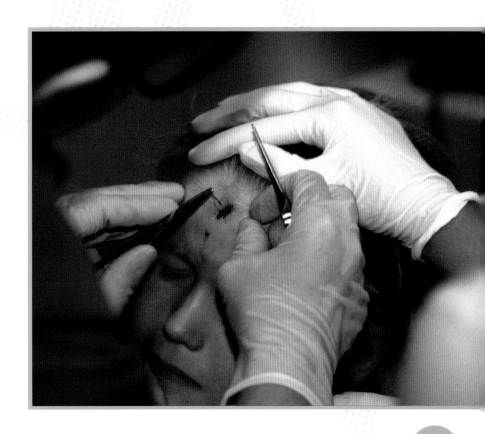

How do cuts heal?

A **scab** forms over the cut and protects it while the cut heals.

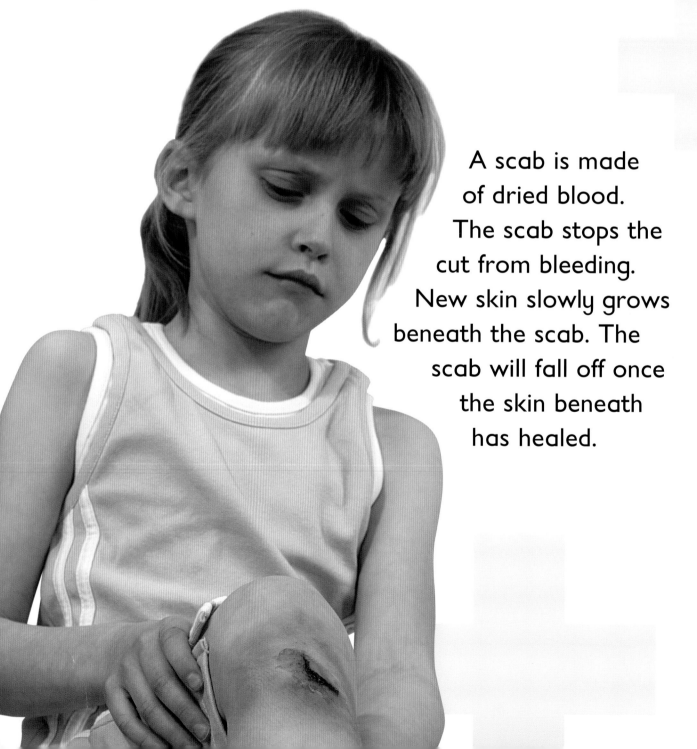

A scab is made of dried blood. The scab stops the cut from bleeding. New skin slowly grows beneath the scab. The scab will fall off once the skin beneath has healed.

As the scab falls off,
you can see the
new skin that has
grown over the cut.

How you can help:

+ Never pull or pick off a scab.
This may make the cut beneath
start to bleed again.

What is a bruise?

A hard bang or knock can burst some of the tiny capillaries beneath the skin. This causes a bruise.

Capillaries are very narrow, so only a small amount of blood leaks out of them. The blood spreads into the skin around the knock.

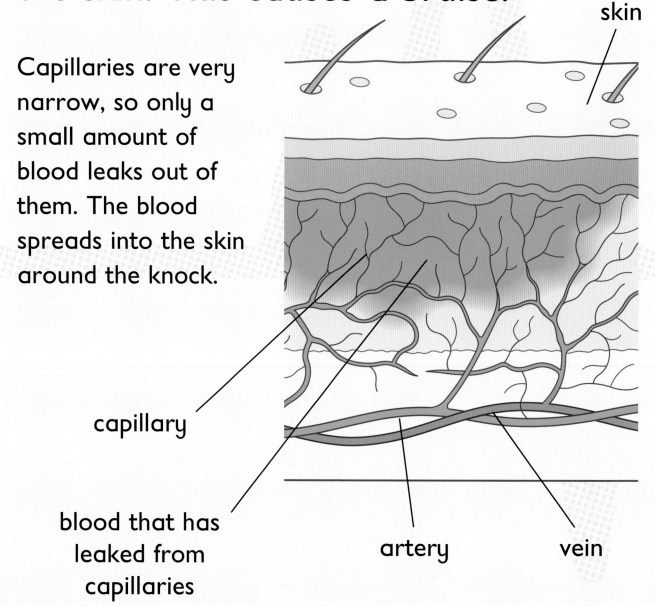

skin

capillary

blood that has leaked from capillaries

artery

vein

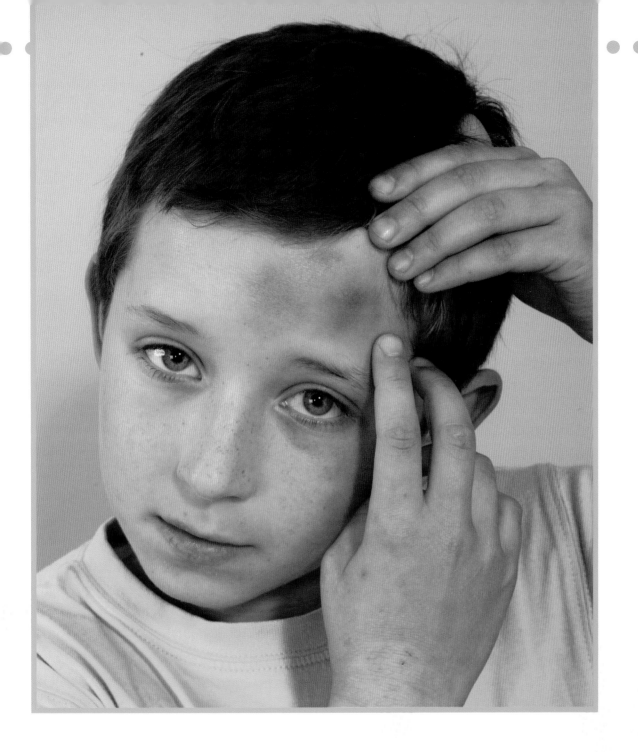

If a knock is very hard, a bump may
also form under the skin. The bump
is caused by flesh swelling up around
the area that has been hurt.

How are bruises treated?

A bruise will slowly heal itself, but using an **ice pack** can help to bring down the swelling.

An ice pack helps to stop a bruise from swelling. It also stops it hurting so much. The ice pack should be used as soon as possible after knocking or bumping the skin.

As a bruise heals, it changes colour. At first the skin turns red. It then changes to purple or black. As it heals, the bruise may turn green and yellow before it fades away.

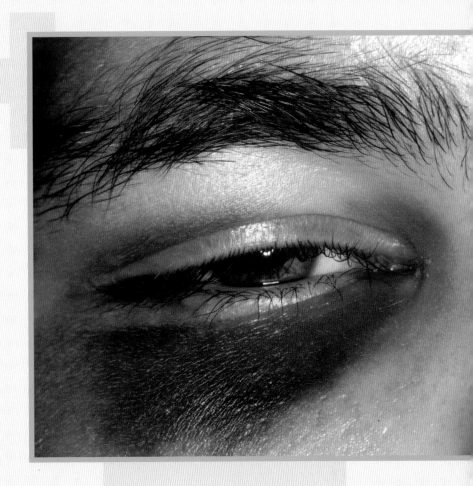

Try this!

+ If you have a bruise, wrap a packet of frozen peas in a tea cloth to make an ice pack.
+ Hold it on the bruise for about 15 minutes to stop it hurting.

What are bones?

Bones are the hard parts inside your body. They make a strong frame called your **skeleton**.

Your skeleton gives your body its shape. Bones also protect your heart and other important parts of your body.

Bones are alive. They are fed by blood, just like the rest of your body.

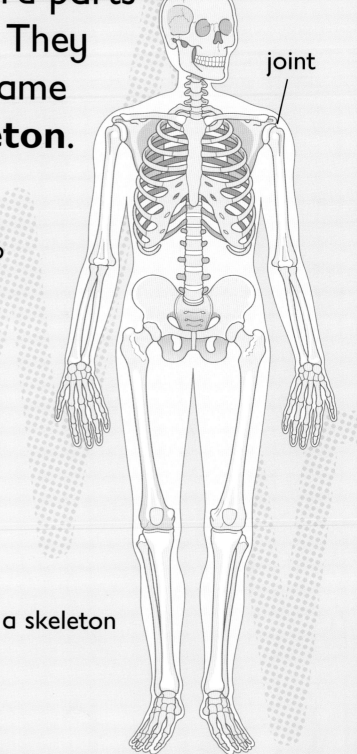

joint

a skeleton

You move your body with the **muscles** attached to your bones. When a bone is broken, it is much harder to move it. A joint is where two bones meet. Your shoulder is a joint. If it is hurt it is hard to move your arm.

Try this!

If you grip your arm tightly, you can feel the bone and muscles beneath your skin!

What happens when a bone is broken?

When a bone is broken, it cracks. It may even break into two or more pieces.

A bad fall can break one or more bones. If you think you may have broken a bone, you should go to hospital for an **X-ray**.

What else are X-rays used for:

X-rays can also be used to look at these other parts of the body:

+ Teeth.
+ Heart.

+ Joints.
+ **Lungs**.

An X-ray is a special photograph of your bones. An X-ray will show if a bone is broken.

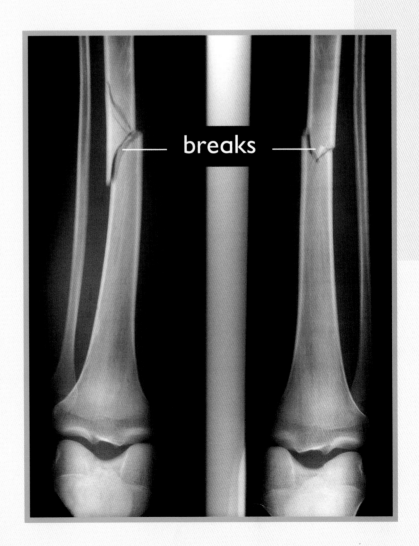

breaks

How are broken bones treated?

A broken bone is put in a cast to protect it while it heals. The cast holds the bone in place.

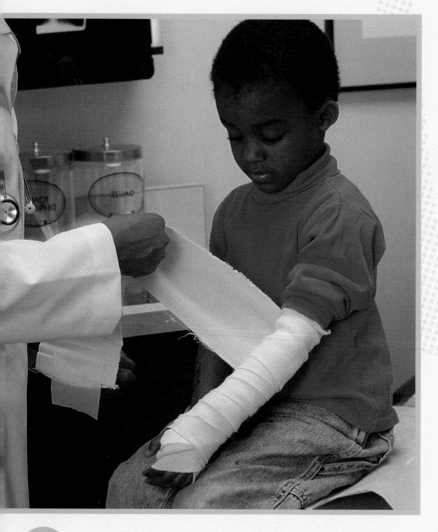

A cast is made from a special **bandage**. The bandage contains **plaster** or **fibreglass**. The bandage is made wet and then wrapped around the bone. As the bandage dries, it becomes hard and strong.

This man has broken his leg. He is wearing a special cast shoe to keep his leg cast off the ground. He must rest his leg and not put any weight on it. His **crutches** take his weight instead.

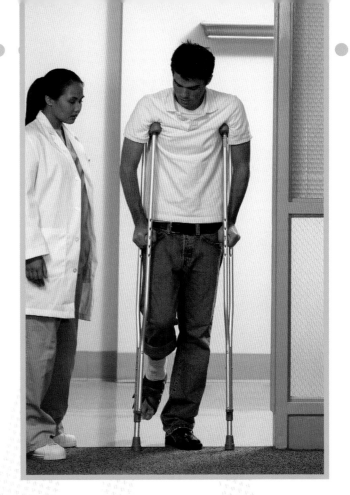

How to take care of a cast:

+ Keep your cast dry. Cover it with a plastic bag when you shower or bath and keep it out of the water.
+ Don't push anything under the cast to scratch an itch. This can make the skin bleed.
+ Do not put talcum powder into your cast. It could make any itching worse.

How do broken bones heal?

Blood fills the gap in the bone where it has broken. New bone slowly grows across the gap.

Along with blood, **marrow** oozes into the break in the bone. New bone slowly grows from the ends of the bones until it closes the gap. The new bone becomes as hard and strong as the rest of the bone.

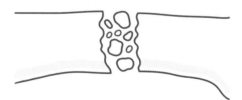

1. The bone breaks.

3. New bone grows.

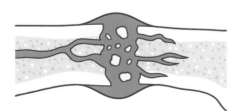

2. Blood and marrow fill the break.

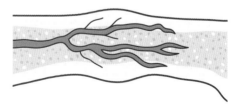

4. The bone heals and becomes strong.

Weak muscles

If someone's arm or leg is in plaster for many weeks, the muscles in that arm or leg become weak. Special exercises will make the muscles strong again.

It can take six or eight weeks for a bone to mend. Once it has healed, the plaster cast is taken off. A special machine cuts through the plaster to remove the cast, but does not touch the skin beneath.

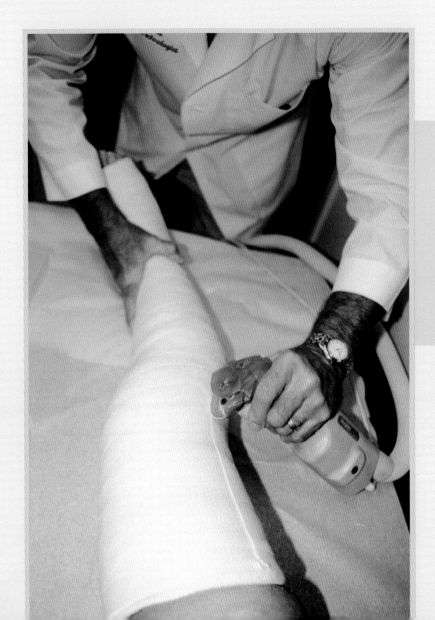

How can injuries be prevented?

You can avoid injuries by being careful, and wearing protective clothes when playing sports.

Sharp knives and scissors can easily cut you. If you need to use a sharp knife or pair of scissors to cut something, ask an adult to help you or to do it for you.

It is easy to fall when you are roller blading or cycling. Always wear a helmet to protect your head. You can also wear special pads on your knees and elbows to protect them if you fall.

How you can help:

+ Old people can easily break a bone if they fall. Tidy the floor before an old person comes to your home.
+ Don't leave toys or things on the floor that people might trip over.

Glossary

antiseptic   stops germs from growing in number.

artery   tube that takes blood from the heart to other parts of the body.

bandage   long strip of fabric that is wrapped around an injury.

capillary   narrow tube that carries blood.

cast   hard covering that protects a broken bone as it heals.

crutches   sticks that support a person while they walk.

fibreglass   material made with very fine strands of glass that is strong but light.

germs   tiny living things that can make you ill.

heal   to get better.

heart   part of the body that pumps blood around the body.

ice pack   freezing cold pack used to lessen injury swelling.

injury   when the body is hurt or damaged.

lung   part of the body that breathes in and breathes out air.

marrow   jelly in the centre of some bones.

muscles   stretchy parts of the body that move our bones.

plaster   a white powder which, when mixed with water, becomes very hard, rigid and strong.

scab   crust of dried blood that covers a cut or wound.

skeleton   all the bones in the body.

stitch   to sew.

vein   tube that carries blood back to the heart.

wound   injury to the skin.

X-ray   special picture of the inside of a body.

Find out more

Take a look at this fun site about broken bones:
www.kidshealth.org/kid/ill_injure/aches/
broken_bones.html

Find out about cuts and scratches:
www.kidshealth.org/kid/watch/er/cuts.html

A children's website about bruises:
www.kidshealth.org/kid/talk/qa/bruise.html

Every effort has been made by the Publisher to ensure that these websites contain no
inappropriate or offensive material. However, because of the nature of the Internet,
it is impossible to guarantee that the contents of these sites will not be altered.
We strongly advise that Internet access is supervised by a responsible adult.

Index

30